The
Unauthorised Collection
of
John Kaldor

The Unauthorised Collection of John Kaldor
Copyright © 2012 by David De Boer
Los Angeles, CA
www.davidmichaeldeboer.com
ISBN 978-1-105-84158-3

Created by David De Boer with contributions from
Andrea Bronte, Mary Coyne and Joseph G. Cruz.

Special Thanks to the Following Supporters

FELT Space - Adelaide, Australia.

Heather and Isabella,
Joseph G. Cruz, Andrea Bronte, Mary Coyne, Steve De Vries,
Dr. Nizan Shaked, Mark Ruwedel, Fran Siegel,
Anthony Creeden, Thomas Murphy, Michael McGregor,
Albert Hwang, James L Marshall, Logan Macdonald, Ray Harris,
Riley O'Keeffe, Polly Dance, Celeste Aldahn, Patrick Rees,
Michael Wunderley, Letty Wunderley, Aaron Giesel,
Ed Giardina, Christen Sperry-Garcia, McLean Fahnestock,
Jerry Donaldson, Marco Cisneros, Huy Dang, Elizabeth Ashline,
Eamonn Fox, Mary Grace Sanchez, Brian Kresge,
Glenn Mobley, Scott Rodgers, Kendra Bosscher, Steve Knapp,
Lee and Michele De Boer, Michael Gallagher, Annelise Soares,
Alison O'Daniel, Marc Steen, Travis J. Barr, Rose Hansaward,
Matthew Winkler, Beau Basse, Carla Duarte, Jocelyn Foye,
Steve Voskanian, Ian Larson, Alan De Boer, Darren Holmes,
Sharon Van Aalsburg, Christopher Smith,
Logan Alvis, Tonya Dantuma

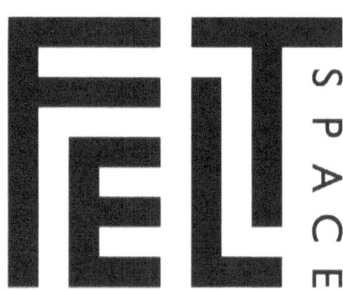

The
Unauthorised Collection
of
John Kaldor

"I.
(EXHORTATION)
MEMORANDUM
DATE: April 6th
TO: Staff
FROM: Todd Birnie
RE: March Performance Stats

I would not like to characterize this as a plea, but it may start to sound like one (!) The fact is, we have a job to do, we have tacitly agreed to do it (did you cash your last paycheck, I know I did, ha ha ha). We have also—to go a step further here—agreed to do the job well. Now we all know that one way to do a job poorly is to be negative about it. Say we need to clean a shelf. Let's use that example. If we spend the hour before the shelf-cleaning talking down the process of cleaning the shelf, complaining about it, dreading it, investigating the moral niceties of cleaning the shelf, whatever, then what happens is, we make the process of cleaning the shelf more difficult than it really is. We all know very well that that "shelf" is going to be cleaned, given the current climate, either by you or by the guy who replaces you and gets your paycheck, so the question boils down to: Do I want to clean it happy or do I want to clean it sad? Which would be more effective? For me? Which would accomplish my purpose more efficiently? What is my purpose? To get paid. How do I accomplish that purpose most efficiently? I clean that shelf well and I clean it quickly. And what mental state helps me clean that shelf well and quickly? Is the answer: Negative? A negative mental state? You know very well that it is not. So the point of this memo is: Positive. The positive mental state will help you clean that shelf well and quickly, and thus accomplish your purpose of getting paid…..

Look, my guys are tired, this is hard work we do, both physically and psychologically. And at that point, at Sectional, believe me, the silence was deafening. And I mean deafening. And the looks I got were not good. And I was reminded, in no uncertain terms, by Hugh Blanchert himself, that our numbers are not to go down. And I was asked to remind you—to remind us, all of us, myself included—that if we are unable to clean our assigned "shelf," not only will someone else be brought in to clean that "shelf," but we ourselves may find ourselves on that "shelf," being that "shelf," with someone else exerting themselves with good positive energy all over us. And at that time I think you can imagine how regretful you would feel, the regret would show in your faces, as we sometimes witness, in Room 6, that regret on the faces of the "shelves" as they are "cleaned," so I am asking you, from the hip, to try your best and not end up a "shelf" which we, your former colleagues, will have no choice but to clean clean clean using all our positive energy, without looking back,…

Todd Birnie
Divisional Director"[1]

-Joseph G. Cruz

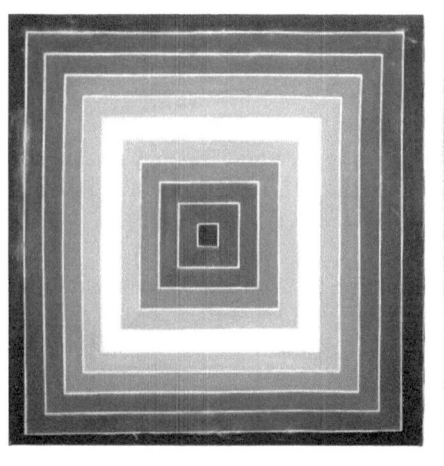 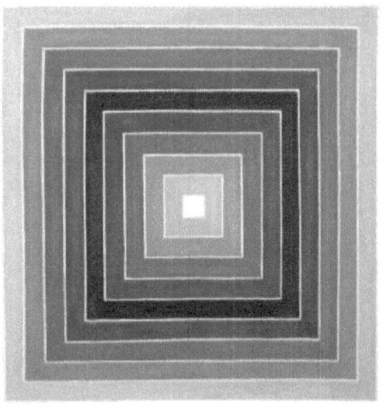

Untitled by Frank Stella 1965, 2012
Oil on canvas (stretched)
82.8 x 162.56 cm[1]

"In the 1950s and 60s Frank Stella was a leading advocate for American art-ists who were attempting to break with the tradition of European painting that made reference to the world of visual effects beyond the canvas and beyond art. Stella wanted to make an art form that was complete in itself, with as little internal division of its form as possible. His early paintings were determined by certain givens, such as the width of the canvas or paintbrush, or the nature of the paint itself. Stella said he wanted to 'keep the paint as good as it was in the can'. He had a favourite house-painting brush 2¾ inches wide and stretched his canvas over stretcher bars that were also 2¾ inches wide – both determining the width of the stripes painted parallel to the stretcher. This structural premise can be considered as the trigger for American minimalism."[2]

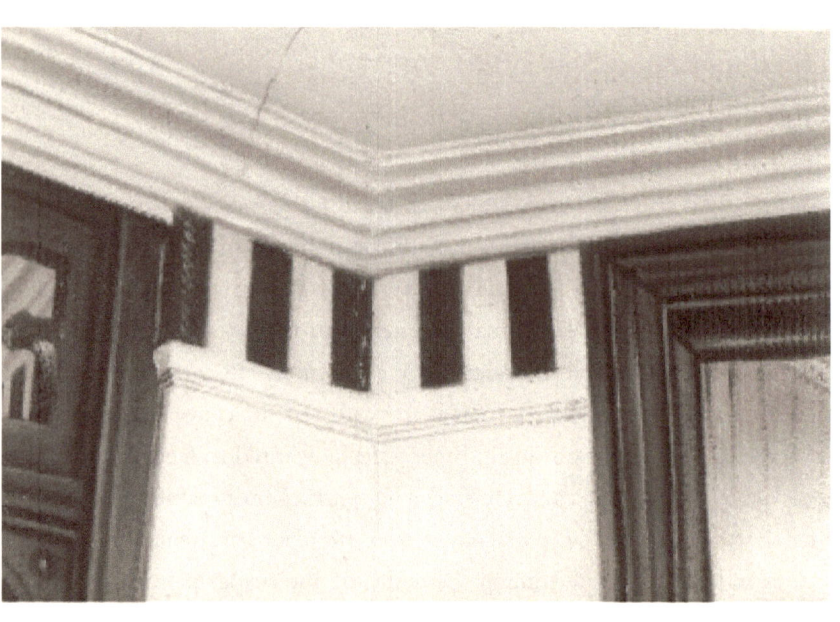

Frise by Daniel Buren 1979, 2012
Oil on canvas (stretched)
5.08 x 12.7 cm^3

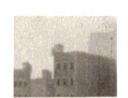 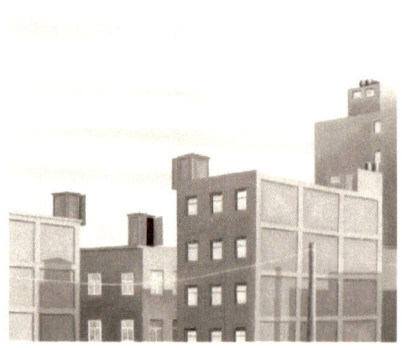 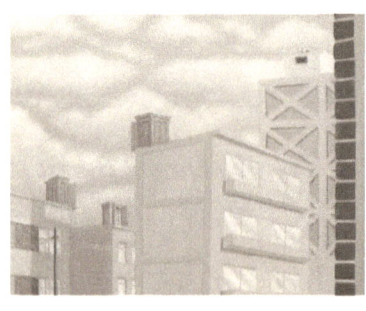

New York triptych by Francis Alÿs 1995-1996, 2012
Oil on canvas (stretched)
6.98 x 8.89 cm, 45.72 x 58.42 cm, 30.38 x 38.1 cm[4]

"Francis Alÿs' work is at once surreal and anchored in everyday experiences of city life. Much of his work occurs in or directly references urban streets and has a peculiar, awkward charm that highlights the strangeness of the ordinary.

'New York triptych' draws upon the vernacular of Mexican sign painting, blurring the boundaries between commercial and fine art practices. Taking up the themes of repetition and authenticity, these works are collaborative, with Alÿs making a small painting that local sign painters then reproduce on a larger scale, each painter inevitably imbuing the image with their own subtle shifts in style and scale."[5]

PAINTING

PAINT ON METAL

168 X 237.6 CM

Painting (1) by Michael Landy 2007, 2012
Oil on canvas (stretched)
83.82 x 116.84 cm[6]

"In typically large-scale ambitious projects, Michael Landy has examined what we value and what we discard, consumerism and waste, and human labour and its worth. His projects – often one-off temporary events – are usually several years in the planning, during which time Landy produces drawings, collages and other related works in which he develops his ideas and processes prior to realising the final work. Landy's practice stands out for its serious consideration of the social structures that determine worth at a basic level of consumption, monetary exchange and employment.

In the 'No frills' series art is reduced to self-descriptive consumer units re-calling the most literal conceptual art practices. The works are as obvious as they appear; there is no more to them than what you see. But of course they also suggest the contested terrain of marketing-fed consumer desire versus consumer rights for low-cost alternatives to branded products. Within the context of the art market this series is a deeply ironic swipe at what the art-world values and why, and the artist as a brand."[7]

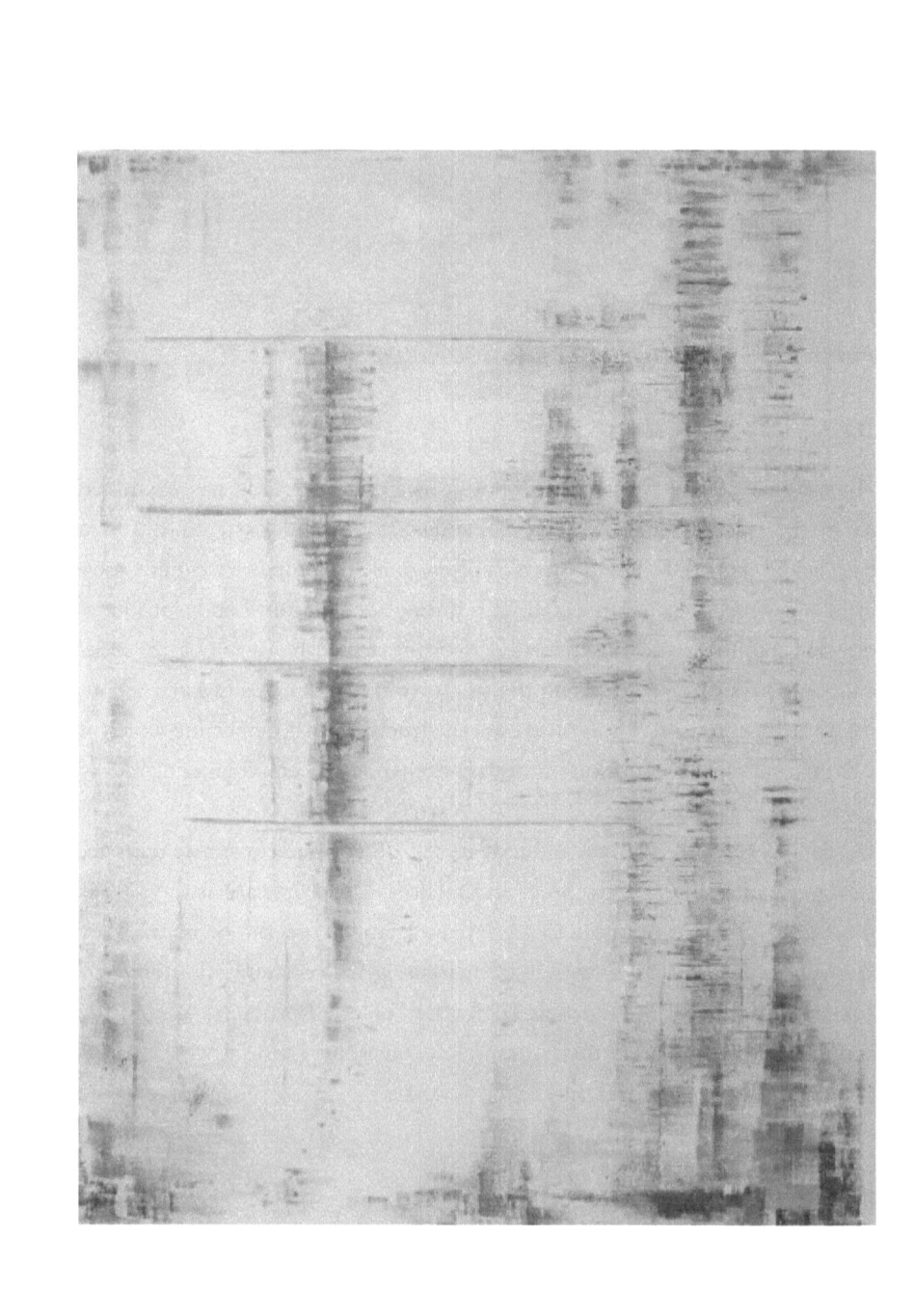

Abstract painting (812) by Gerhard Richter 1994, 2012
Oil on canvas (stretched)
121.92 x 96.52 cm[8]

"Richter's early paintings gave Pop Art a political edge. His subject matter was often based on news print photographs mimicking the blurring of surveillance images taken from a moving car. Richter's origins in Eastern Germany gave this quality a more personal resonance. His painting's relationship to photography has remained constant even though his subject matter has varied from landscape, to historical paintings, to apparently minimalist abstraction. It is not the accuracy of the image that interests him but on the contrary the potential for blurring, loss of focus and definition that it produces.

In his installation 'Atlas' at DIA in New York and later at Documenta 1997 Richter displayed a vast array of small photos taken as if for a sketchbook. These included hundreds of images of textures, clouds, seas, tiles, brickwork, trees, and so on. These were sometimes painted over, sometimes re-photographed so that the layering of photograph and paint became inextricably conflated. The textures and colours of the worked photos bore a striking resemblance to the repertoire of marks and colours of Richter's abstract paintings.

This repertoire is translated into a painterly tradition that is connected to Titian and Velasquez and so through Monet to Rothko. This tradition is partially expressed in the Baroque tendency to break the surface of the paint and blur the image to stimulate imaginative interpretation by the viewer. In spite of his relation to tradition, Richter has one strong affiliation with Minimalism. He emphasises process and paint as stuff rather than as a medium for pictorial composition. This is particularly evident in the abstractions where the paint is dragged onto the canvas with a squeegee. In 'Abstract painting (812)' he has used only one colour in the over painting, it has been dragged across the stretched canvas on which an earlier darker composition had been laid down. In the process he emphasises the underlying materiality of painting by revealing the horizontal stretcher bars. The rich yellow of this top coat produces a summery, buttery, glow. This glow is accentuated by glimpses of the underpainting that hint at deep space beyond the surface and as electric flashes against the yellow."[9]

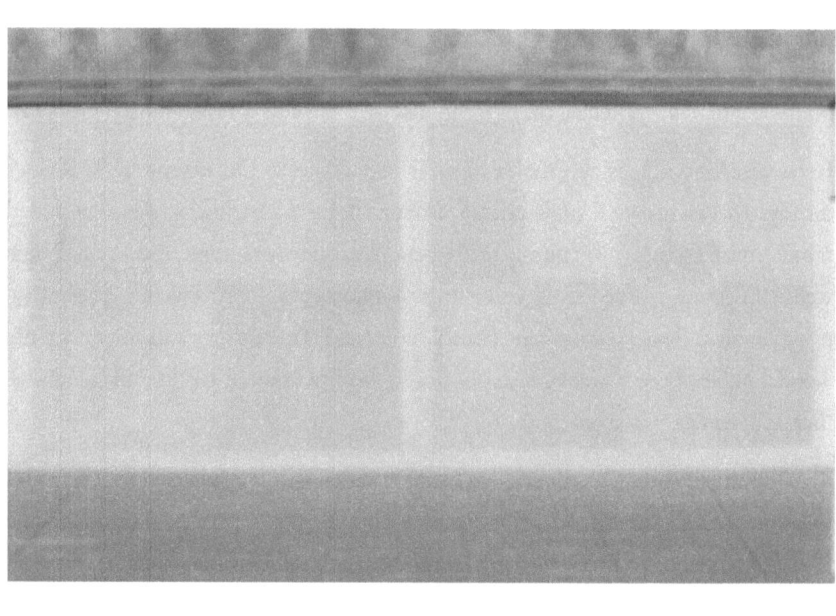

Wall drawing #337: two part wall drawing. The wall is divided vertically into two parts. Each part is divided horizontally and vertically into four equal parts. 1st part: lines in four directions, one direction in each quarter. 2nd part: lines in four directions, superimposed progressively and Wall drawing #338: two part wall drawing. The wall is divided vertically into two parts. Each part is divided horizontally and vertically into four equal parts. 1st part: lines in four directions, one direction in each quarter. 2nd part: lines in four directions, superimposed progressively by Sol Lewitt 1971, 2012
Oil on canvas (stretched)
20.32 x 30.48 cm[10]

"First Drawn by: Kazuko Miyamoto
First Installation: Panza di Biumo residence, Varese, Italy, June 1980

Sol LeWitt's wall drawings are executed by professional draughts people from sets of instructions generated by the artist. LeWitt emphasised the idea or concept of an artwork over its visual realisation, hence his assertion that his instructions are themselves the work of art.

'Wall drawing #337' and 'Wall drawing #338' exemplify this process: both works are drawn by professional draughtspeople following LeWitt's instructions. The artist's methodology has been likened to that of a composer: the works are manifested by others, and no single drawing is ever the definitive version. In a 1971 interview LeWitt commented: 'I try to make the plan specific enough so that it comes out more or less how I want it, but general enough that [the draughtspeople] have the freedom to interpret. It's as though I am writing of piece of music and somebody else is going to play it on the piano.'[11]

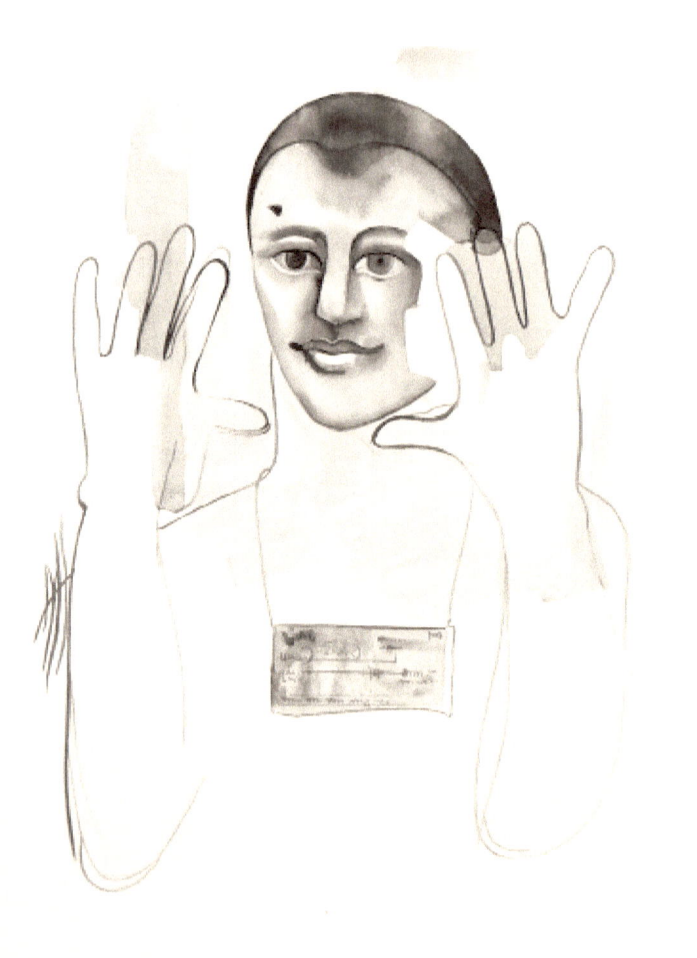

Untitled (hippie drawing) by Richard Prince 2000-2005, 2012
Mixed media on paper (framed)
50.8 x 38.1 cm[12]

Mary Coyne

Alive and Well: The Role of the Author

In a prophesizing article published in the *Stanford Law Review* in 1996, Keith Aoki stated that laws regarding intellectual property in the U.S. were haunted by "a romantic vision of originary authorship that is deeply embedded in the national intellectual property regimes of Western Europe and North America."[i] Although approaching the situation from a strictly legal perspective, Aoki addressed an issue subversive in art historical discourse since Walter Benjamin's call for art's proletarianism in the 1930s.[ii] Since then, the idea of the author as creator and premier generator of meaning for a work has been fundamentally questioned and challenged. In the last decade, the forces of globalization, digital networks combined with the flexuous global market have impacted the steadfast role of the author.

Post-Structuralist thought has already challenged the role of author, with Roland Barthes famously pronouncing his death in 1967.[iii] Barthes' proclamation of the "Death of the Author" came at a time when the Cartesian individual was being deconstructed from multiple angles. The ideas of self expression formerly associated with the author (or artist) were reconsidered, and as Barthes articulated, all "expression" was no more than an arrangement of ever shifting signs.[iv] Where Barthes handily replaced the author with the reader as generator of meaning, this substitution was not enough for Michel Foucault.[v] Instead, Foucault emphasized that we must go beyond the realization that the author is dead, emphasizing that his absence opens up a space into which new possibilities may occur. Such a space has emerged with the expansion of the Internet, yet forty years after his writing, the author still maintains many of its former holds on the work attached to it, and due to the advent of late Capitalism, has even developed more value and power.

Internet sharing and licensing has, in the last decade renewed the need to reconsider the author.[vi]   In the twenty-first-century, retaining authourtorial status has become a struggle; the rights and privileges traditionally bestowed upon that title are grounds for contention, debate and ambiguity. The value of texts, music, entire bodies of work are undermined as they are shared digitally and through blogs, vlogs and YouTube; millions of voices have a equal opportunity to develop and communicate their ideas. Yet the role of author has not diminished through this multiplicity and democratization, instead, it seems to be even more valued and staked as title and claim.

Antonio Calcagno, in his reading of Derrida as author vis-à-vis a Foucaultian theorization of the term, argues that despite the fact that deconstruction largely re-evaluates and questions the authority of the "author" or artist figure, Derrida still affixed his own name to his texts.[vii] The reluctance of the author figure to relinquish his "author function" derives from the power the role holds, an aspect highlighted by Foucault.

> "the author is not an indefinite source of significations which fill a work; the author does not precede the works; he is a certain functional principle by which, in our culture, one limits, excludes, and chooses; in short, by which one impedes the free circulation, the free manipulation, the free composition, decomposition, and recomposition of fiction. . . One can say that the author is an ideological product, since we represent him as the opposite of his historically real function." [viii]

Because the author's name substitutes for the work produced by that name, both the work and the name are provided with a reciprocal value. As author, an artist like John Baldessari has the ability to control, to some extent, the ways in which his work is understood, the channels through which it circulates, the discourses in which it enters and—as the original owner of an individual object—the hands into which it passes. Although it seems obvious on one level, the author's name signifies beyond the original product. The name "Baldessari" indicates more than the physical paint on the canvas but also the vast discourse surrounding it, the theoretical implications of the work and even, for some, Conceptualism as a movement. Considering this, the artist's choice to affix his own name to the work points to both the inherent paradoxes in his own practice, but more importantly for the question of authorship— the highly desirable status of, and thus, the challenges to eradicate, the role of author. Baldessari's practice, which utilizes mechanized, stencil text, appropriated images and engages a biting critique of the art market and artistic conventions, antagonizes the bundle of conventions attached to the concept of author. Yet by constructing a cohesive "body of work" that can be signified by his own name, Baldessari maintains his ability to conceptually as well as legally maintain power over his practice. The perceived value of the work itself, conversely grants Baldessari, as an acclaimed artist, power, privileges and self-identity.

Examined in the present media-saturated cultural situation, the idea of "author" emerges as that which is clung to as the last stake in identity. The Pop artists of the 1960s pointed to an acute self-consciousness of the waning of identity, a sentiment that could only expand exponentially by the current age.[ix] It is this desire for the validation of our names that is in part responsible for the worldwide blogging and social media phenomena as we almost frantically generate work in order to file it under our names, ever expanding our status as author. The knowledge of being one voice of millions, reiterates the need to preserve at least some semblance of identity of that voice.

There is an even stronger system of supports of the author than a reluctance to deny the ego. As Barthes indicated, the rise of late capitalism placed even further importance to the 'person' of the author as generator of value. In the same way that the author controls his work, he also lends his name as a signifier of value to it and its adjacent discourse or, in post-late capitalism, the objects surrounding it. Identified by Isabelle Graw in her book, *High Price*, the "cult of celebrity" illustrates the way in which celebrity personas have become the end goal for the artist and contemporary culture.[x] The act of producing with the aim of being "discovered" is one of the largest roadblocks to the eradication of the role of the author. Such a commercial value intertwined with the author function is one that had not yet been fully realized at the time of Barthes or even Foucault's writings. The material aspect of the role of author, now oddly absent from their texts cannot be separated from the privileges of power surrounding authorship. This amplified value of the artist's name, which has of late reached a point where mere appearances by the celebrity of interest demand six-figure sums. Yet the value of the name is nothing new, it relies on conventions tied to the author almost since its establishment on the heels of the Enlightenment. [xi] In December 2011, Knoedler Gallery in New York was forced to close after they sold a later-exposed imposter Jackson Pollock painting for seventeen million dollars.[xii] This latest event in the chain of controversies and legal battles surrounding "fakes" as counterfeiters swarm to respond to the demand of the surging art market.[xiii] For the unfortunate buyer, a few million was a fair transaction for the Pollock name; without his verification of artistic excellence or economic value, the painting was rendered worthless. With the author's name so intrinsically connected to the work's value, his proverbial death or regeneration seems more and more unlikely in the face of current market values. Where textual materials, music and video have all proven to be comparatively dispensable in their ability to be accessed outside the controlling channels of the author, art has remained largely singular and thus dependent on the author/artist.

Treatment of the artist is thus inextricable from traditional, even "romantic" idealizations of the author function. Art, its reception, display and market rely almost entirely on the connection to its creator. Despite theoretical re-definitions, cultural and technological changes, the author has proven steadfast, and has, despite the ultimate challenge of the Internet maintained a status of power. The fact that there was few alterations made to the laws concerning art since the advent of the Internet, as there have been to other intellectual property and copyrighted materials signifies that the art world has some catching up to do. Despite the roadblocks indicated above, it is on its way. Culturally, the expectation of a singular author with supreme authority of a work is diminishing. Internet art, interventions, and Public Art all to some extent subvert the reliance of the author as authoritative generator of meaning and context. Digitally we are able to manipulate others' works of art, decontextualize and encounter them outside what may be considered the accepted paradigms. These examples describe something like Foucault's space left by the author, ripe for more creative authorship. Such a space transcends the physical limitations of text and allows interaction with the author as a theoretical tool for expansion, testing and even manipulation.

Andrea Bronte

In The Eye of The Beholder:
Artistic Value and Censorship[1]

"Every man knows where and how beauty gives him pleasure."
~ John Ruskin, The Lamp of Beauty

Historically, art museums are highly politicized environments that have been used as vehicles through which societal and cultural issues are explored and debated. Included in those debates, censorship in the arts has been enacted from within and without the museum institution. A core issue of arts censorship is the determination of artistic value. In this essay, I will explore how and by whom artistic value is determined and how it is related to censorship in the arts. I will look comparatively at two artworks whose artistic value is undetermined based on an inability to authenticate them. In support of my research I will broadly examine the history surrounding the attempts to authenticate each of the works; legal determinations of artistic authenticity; definitions of aesthetic value; aesthetics and connoisseurship and museum history and museological practices.

In 1985, The Getty Museum acquired what they strongly believed was a 6th century B.C.E. archaic Greek Kouros for 9.5 million dollars. The purchase of the object was made with the understanding that its authenticity could not be validated at the time, nor later could its provenance.[2] Fourteen months prior to and eighteen months after its purchase were spent on various scientific and stylistic examinations in an attempt to authenticate the object.[3] At present, the "artwork" is on view at the Getty Villa Malibu. The Getty website publicizes the object with information that reads as follows:

Statue of a Kouros
Unknown
Greek, about 530 B.C., or modern forgery
Marble
81 1/8 x 21 ½ in.[4]

A portion of the accompanying website text reads:

> Neither art historians nor scientists have been able to completely resolve the issue of the Getty Museum kouros's authenticity. Certain elements of the statue have led to this questioning, especially a mixture of earlier and later stylistic traits and the use of marble from the island of Thasos at a date when its use is unexpected. Yet the anomalies of the Getty kouros may be due more to our limited knowledge of Greek sculpture in this period rather than to mistakes on the part of a forger.[5]

The information, documentation, and evidence surrounding the exhibition of the Getty Kouros provide a context for understanding the complex dynamics of authenticating (and in turn, evaluating) an artwork. What is interesting in this case is twofold. First, the Getty museum is perceived as a well-respected art institution, whose financial and personnel resources contribute to significant scholarship in the arts. By reputation alone–although the Getty has been involved in questionable activities in the past–the museum has the authority and power to authenticate, or discredit, art objects that fall within their areas of specialization.[6] Of secondary interest, is that although museums have been historically perceived as places that present information as fact, the Getty Museum, endowed with authorial license, is able to and willingly does exhibit its Kouros for academic study, even though its authenticity and by extension its *value*, is inconclusive.[7]

In contrast to the Getty Kouros, is a painting presumed by its owner Teri Horton, to be a Jackson Pollock. (For the purposes of this discussion, I will hereby refer to the painting as the Horton Pollock.) In an effort to maintain an equitable inquiry, a brief outline of Horton's background is in order. Horton is a retired truck driver with an eighth-grade education and no formal art education or professional experience evaluating or authenticating artworks. Purchased at a thrift store for five dollars and later thought to be a Jackson Pollock, Horton enlisted the expert assistance of various individuals in an effort to authenticate the painting - none have been able to conclusively prove that the Horton Pollock was created "by the hand of Pollock."[8] Nevertheless, Horton maintains that the painting is indeed a Pollock and has actively pursued its authentication with the intention of selling it. Unlike the Getty Kouros however, the authenticity of the Horton Pollock is not the primary issue at stake. In the case of the Horton Pollock, connoisseurship (and its attendant privileges) is the dominant issue. Because Horton lacks access to the mechanisms of power needed to authenticate her artwork, she does not have the privilege the Getty has had in creating its own self-sustaining agency.

The issues of authentication for both the Getty Kouros and Horton Pollock are the same. Both objects have undergone extensive scientific and scholarly review; both works are of questionable provenance, and both cannot be proven to be "genuine." What is different however is that the Getty, by name, is endowed as an accredited art institution working in the service of public good and scholarly research, whose artworks, as cultural patrimony, are exhibited as standards of artistic excellence and value. In contrast, Horton is a self-appointed art connoisseur with no name (provenance), no social status, no art experience and no interest in the artwork other than for personal financial gain. Speaking on behalf of the Fine Art Registry in regard to Horton, Cindy Hill, Esq. commented:

> In the field of art authentication, it's important to remember first off that most questions of art identification do not go to court. Rather, they are 'tried' in the court of public opinion and media, and ultimately in the marketplace with the question of whether a buyer is willing to believe or not believe the

identification being offered by the seller. Ms. Horton has pre-
sented her painting to this court of public opinion…. as such,
she has made herself a 'public figure' and the identification a
matter of public interest; therefore comments on her painting
and its identification are matters of Constitutionally protected
First Amendment free speech. In other words, because she has
sought the public limelight, voicing an opinion on Ms. Horton's
identification of this painting is fair ground for public debate.
Within this realm of public opinion, the Rules of Evidence do
not apply.[9]

Although the Getty has not "sought the public limelight" with their
Kouros, they are a public entity. However, because the Getty has not placed
the Kouros' authenticity within the "court of public opinion," its legitimacy
(by Ms. Hill's interpretation of the law) *can* be determined using scientific
evidence and does not fall under the same evaluations as the Horton Pollock. Conversely, because Horton *has* placed her issue within the court of
public opinion, she has (by Hill's interpretation of the law) eliminated the
possibility of using evidence to prove the authenticity of her artwork. Beyond legal determinations of authenticity, a central difference between the
Getty Kouros and the Horton Pollock are the elaborate social mechanisms
by which artworks are evaluated and the subsequent censorious reverbera-
tions that affect their reception and interpretation in the pubic sphere.

In the case of the Horton Pollock, issues of authenticity are secondary to Horton's art expertise (or lack thereof.) Horton places her opinion equal among those more practiced in the field, however she does so
under the exclusive purview of connoisseurship. Used to determine artistic
value and defined as a person who is especially competent to pass critical
judgments in art, particularly of the fine arts, or in matters of taste. Writing
about value and easily applied to the definition of connoisseurship, Joseph
Leo Koerner and Lisbet Rausing state, "the source of value lay not in the
judged object but in the judging subject."[10] Here is where issues of class
and privilege directly inform determinations of value. Summarizing Pierre

Bourdieu, Koerner and Rausing state:

> Value *seems* to be a judgment made freely by the individual in his
> or her irreducible subjectivity, and good taste appears therefore
> to be a natural proclivity. *In fact*, these are ways of maintain-
> ing social distinctions by masking the real privileges that enable
> judgments in the first place. Here we encounter one 'objective'
> approach to the subjective value of art, for it discerns in the
> realm of the aesthetic, and in the value of privacy and subjec-
> tivity cultivated there, the social negotiation of power.[11]

I would agree with Bourdieu that evaluative judgments of artistic
merit and aesthetic value offer very little objectivity on the part of the evalu-
ator, or that which is evaluated. In addition, assessments of aesthetic value,
made by a "qualified" connoisseur are largely mediated through socioeconomic factors such as race, class, and wealth, all of which are arbitrary designations of social privilege. It is through the access to and production of
social privilege, that censorship is activated. By its very nature and practice,
connoisseurship is exclusionary. In the case of the connoisseur as an evaluating subject, by virtue of their socioeconomic status, there are individuals
and institutions that are granted access to the world of social distinction (of
which the arts are included) and others, who are not.

The complex relationship between connoisseurship and social privilege are pivotal in both the Getty Kouros and the Horton Pollock. Horton's social credentials were broadcasted through various film, television and
print stories of her and her painting. All focused on Horton's (lack of) social status, some to greater or lesser extent. Some reporting was particularly
nasty. Randy Kennedy for *The New York Times* called Horton "a sandpaper-
voiced woman with a hard-shell perm who lives in a mobile home in Costa
Mesa and depends on her Social Security checks."[12] In the documentary
about Horton, *Who the #$&%% is Jackson Pollock?*, the controversial Thomas
Hoving former director of The Metropolitan Museum of Art, stated (about
Horton), after having inspected the painting, "she knows nothing–I'm an

expert, she's not."[13]   Hoving then cast his connoisseurial "expertise" into the realm of gender studies in an article for artnet, calling Horton a "gritty, retired eighteen-wheeler-driver," which could be read as an attempt to discredit her as a female and thereby remove the one thing that may afford her (perceived) agency.[14]   The Getty institution on the other hand, though it did draw much criticism in the press for its cavalier handling of the Kouros acquisition, and later for the artwork's dubious provenance that pointed to administrative racketeering–which provoked the resignation of the antiquities curator who brokered the acquisition–did not suffer Horton's public humiliation. The Getty instead was insulated from any serious censure of its reputation and as a result, the power and authority that validates its agency remained intact. Horton on the other hand, was established in broadcast media as a person who fundamentally lacks the "appropriate" professional, and more importantly *social*, credentials to secure her agency.

In addition to social privilege, connoisseurship imparts value onto the artwork and functions as a representation of the person (or entity) from whom its evaluative judgment has been made. The art object validates (and reflects) the connoisseurship of the owner/beholder. Here, it is useful to consider the insightful Donald Preziosi who describes the art object as a psycho-semiotic object that mirrors back to its (viewing) public all of it's desires and insecurities and I would add, entitlements. He sees the art object as the ultimate reflection of that which society desires to be in its greatest form.[15] Similarly, Andrea Fraser wrote, "art, as legitimate cultural production, serves primarily as the objectified form of the competencies and dispositions of those who consume it, on the one hand, and, on the other, of those who produce it, its discourse, and its practices of consumption."[16]   Once an artwork has received the connoisseur's approval, it then becomes an object to be consumed–visually, intellectually, and emotionally. If the object is a reflection of its validating source, then consuming the object becomes a symbolic substitution for consuming its authorizing entity. In the case of the Horton Pollock - a retired truck driver with an eighth-grade education and no art experience. And in the case of the Getty Kouros - a multi-billion dollar, world-renowned art institution of substantial scholarly and aesthetic import. Seen in this context, it becomes clear why there was such a strong reaction against Teri Horton as self-proclaimed connoisseur. In the words of Hoving speaking about the Horton Pollock, "*it* has no appeal, *it's* dead on arrival."[17] Is Hoving referring to Horton *or* her painting? In this case, what or whom Hoving is speaking about becomes indistinguishable.

The notion of the art object representing its owner was not lost on Horton. It is worthwhile to consider that Horton has had two offers on her painting, which by her own subjective measures she considers to be worth fifty million dollars. After a fingerprint on the back of the Horton Pollock canvas was matched by an art forensics expert to one on a paint can in Pollock's studio, an offer for two million dollars was issued. Horton declined, saying, "it was not a fair offer. Be fair with me and I'll sell it."[18] The second offer, from a Saudi art collector, was for nine million dollars. Horton refused again. In the *Who the #$&%% is Jackson Pollock?* documentary, an off-screen interviewer said, "five dollar investment becomes two million, that's real money." Horton responded, "is it really? Not when you're sitting on principle."[19] But it was her son, who had devoted a great deal of his time to assisting Horton in authenticating the painting, who perceptively remarked, "money has never really been an issue–it's a validation of her."[20] Recalling Koerner and Rausing, Hoving, Preziosi, and Fraser, Horton understands all too well that the Horton Pollock is more than the sum of its parts–it is a reflection of *her*, her social class and worth, her desire for recognition, and, her principle. Because *Horton* lacks the appropriate social and professional credentials, the Horton Pollock is effectively discredited and censored from art world consideration. The Getty Kouros on the other hand, although it exists in an indeterminate state of authenticity, still bears the stamp and reflection of its owner, therefore protecting its aesthetic value and academic reception from censorship.

Designations of aesthetic value and connoisseurship are not objective and it is interesting to consider that the very structures that generate and authorize these privileges have a vested interest in maintaining established mechanisms of power. Fraser states, "refusals to hold and apply specific, articulated criteria often have less to do with maintaining neutrality or defending the free range of artistic experimentation than with protecting the social, economic, and symbolic capital that is usually the true basis, in such cases, for artistic legitimacy."[21] Speaking on the development of symbolic and cultural capital in the history of Western art, Amelia Jones points to the early formations of art's discourse and reception, stating that it's inception was born of a subjective and universalizing, white male hierarchy.[22] Into this discourse, the display and reception of the art object became paramount in the formation of its meaning (value) and in turn, the meaning (value) of it's viewing audience. As a result, the museum, as container of these constructed meanings, was created.[23] Speaking of the power of the early 19th century museum in constructing these dialogues, Tony Bennett wrote, "rather than embodying an alien and coercive principle of power which aimed to cow the people into submission, the museum – addressing the people as a public, as citizens – aimed to inveigle the general populace into complicity with power by placing them on this side of a power which it represented to it as its own."[24] I would argue that not much has changed in the 21st century. Historically, the mechanisms that shape and control an artwork's meaning have in large part been established by Enlightenment era museological practices and museums, as *institutions*. By extension, the professionals who implement such mechanisms are very closely tied to maintaining and establishing said power, however much advances in 20th and 21st century inclusionary museum practices have been made. Therefore, questions of what artworks are chosen for public exhibition and how artworks are received in the public sphere, return us to the Getty Kouros and Horton Pollock.

It is interesting to consider why the Getty chose to exhibit and openly publicize the undetermined authenticity of one of its holdings and how this relates to Horton's predicament. Protected from professional discreditation, the Getty institution possesses the connoisseurship to exhibit its unauthenticated Kouros, whereas Horton possesses no such authority, or power. The Getty has a symbolic investment in its Kouros that exceeds its monetary or aesthetic value, and exhibiting it produces a twofold effect. First, exhibiting the Kouros sculpture and publicizing its undetermined authenticity work to exonerate the bad press and professional demerits the Getty received when the object was acquired and its provenance questioned. Secondly, the Getty has a vested interest in maintaining its status as an institution of cultural authority. By choosing to make transparent the oft times dubious and uncertain nature with which artworks are acquired, even by credited institutions, the Getty maintains control and power over the machinations of *how* aesthetic value and meaning are determined and constructed. Regarding the expertise of art professionals, Fraser wrote, "art professionals have an interest in maintaining and increasing (that is, of reproducing) their monopoly on that competence, an interest that is more or less inseparable from an interest in their professional, social, and historical status."[25] Compared to the Getty, Horton is not burdened with having to explain her painting so much as herself. For Horton it would seem, the "court of public opinion" has judged her value as an individual, precluding her and her painting from serious public consideration. For the Getty, judgment is placed on the object as a symbol of the connoisseur's expertise (or lack thereof) where reparations of its legitimacy are more easily made. Both cases deal with censorship as it relates to determinations of value made by an evaluating subject. However, the Getty has the agency to create and sustain its own meaning and Horton does not.

How then do we level the playing field of how aesthetic value is determined? Is this even possible? Is connoisseurship and the elaborate social mechanisms surrounding the reception and interpretation of art so institutionalized that change is not possible? Is censorship inherent in being a judging subject? To these questions, I would offer that the way in which artwork is evaluated and received in today's world faces multiple, complex challenges. One, as human beings we are by nature subjective, and therefore censorious. Two, humans have institutionalized (and internalized) outmoded art historical canons and museological practices to the extent that they are subconscious, normative, and censorious. Emory Elliott offered the following, "the issue then is not whether we can rid ourselves of the disciplines that address the desire for beauty and art; rather, it must be how to redefine the parameters of "art" and formulate new questions for evaluating cultural expression in ways that are fair and just to all."[26]   Here, I would agree that creating new contexts within which art is received and interpreted could create a more equitable exchange of ideas. Could the Getty's public display of its inconclusive connoisseurship be a move in this direction? Is the "court of public opinion" in Teri Horton's case an opportunity for *everyone* to be involved in the dialogue of what is and is not art, and who determines it? Or, is it just reifying existing power structures? Ultimately, I am most closely aligned with Amelia Jones' thoughts when she wrote: "I hope to suggest a way of evaluating works of art that is more in sync with contemporary politics and culture¬–one that understands rather than veils or occludes the contingency of meaning and value and the role of the interpreter in determining both."[27]

Endnotes:
Prologue / Joseph G. Cruz

[1]   George Saunders, "Four Institutional Monologues," in *Timothy McSweeney's Quarterly Concern*, ed. Dave Eggers, Issue No. 4: *Trying, Trying, Trying, Trying, Trying*, Late Winter (San Francisco, CA: McSweeney's Publishing, 2000), 1,4.

Endnotes:

The Unauthorised Collection of John Kaldor / David De Boer

[1] Representation of Frank Stella's *Untitled* (1965) was fabricated in China at fifty percent scale of the original in oil on unstretched canvas and later stretched for presentation. Details of the original artwork are as follows: Frank Stella, *Untitled* (1965), Synthetic Polymer Paint on Canvas, 160.0 x 320.5 x 7.7 cm. John Kaldor Family Collection at the Art Gallery of New South Wales.

[2] Art Gallery New South Wales, "Frank Stella," http://www.artgallery.nsw.gov.au/work/L2010.73/(accessed May 19, 2012).

[3] Representation of Daniel Buren's *Frise* (1979) was fabricated in China at one hundred percent scale of its digital representation as shown on the Art Gallery of New South Wales website in oil on unstretched canvas and later stretched for presentation. The Art Gallery of New South Wales website does not provide a narrative description about the atwork or artist. Details of the original artwork are as follows: Daniel Buren, *Frise* (1979) installation dimensions variable stripe: 8.7cm wide; 26.1cm height. John Kaldor Family Collection at the Art Gallery of New South Wales.

[4] Representation of Francis Alÿs' *New York triptych* (1995-1996) was fabricated in China at fifty percent scale of the original in oil on unstretched canvas and later stretched for presentation. Details of the original artwork are as follows: Francis Alÿs, *New York triptych (*1995-1996) from the series "Sign Painters project 1993-1997", triptych: oil on canvas, enamel on metal series consisting of one painting by Francis Alÿs and two sign paintings by Enrique Huerta and Emilio Rivera, a) 13.5 x 15.8 x 2.0cm b) 91.0 x 120.0 x 4.0cm c) 60.0 x 75.0 x 2.0cm. John Kaldor Family Collection at the Art Gallery of New South Wales.

[5] Art Gallery New South Wales, "Francis Alÿs," http://www.artgallery.nsw.gov.au/work/L2010.4.a-c/.(accessed May 19, 2012).

[6] Representation of Michael Landy's *Painting (1)* (2007) was fabricated in China at fifty percent scale of the original in oil on unstretched canvas and later stretched for presentation. Details of the original artwork are as follows: Michael Landy, *Painting (1)* (2007) from the series "No frills" (2007) Paint on Metal, 168.0 x 237.6 x 4.0cm. John Kaldor Family Collection at the Art Gallery of New South Wales.

[7] Art Gallery New South Wales, "Michael Landy," http://www.artgallery.nsw.gov.au/work/L2010.47/ (accessed May 19, 2012).

[8] Representation of Gerhard Richter's *Abstract painting (812)* (1994) was fabricated in China at fifty percent scale of the original in oil on unstretched canvas and later stretched for presentation. Details of the original artwork are as follows:

Gerhard Richter, *Abstract painting (812)* (1994) Oil on Canvas, 250.00 x 200.00 cm. John Kaldor Family Collection at the Art Gallery of New South Wales.

[9]   Art Gallery New South Wales, "Gerhard Richter," http://www.artgallery.nsw. gov.au/work/65.1999/ (accessed May 19, 2012).

[10]   Representation of Sol Lewitt's *Wall Drawing #337: Two part drawing. The wall is divided vertically into two parts. Each part is divided horizontally and vertically into four equal parts. 1st part: Lines in four directions, one direction in each quarter. 2nd part: Lines in four directions, superimposed progressively*(1971) and *Wall Drawing #338: Two part drawing. The wall is divided vertically into two parts. Each part is divided horizontally and vertically into four equal parts. 1st part: Lines in four directions, one direction in each quarter. 2nd part: Lines in four directions, superimposed progressively* (1971) was fabricated in China at one hundred percent scale of its digital representation as shown on the Art Gallery of New South Wales website in oil on unstretched canvas and later stretched for presentation. Details of the original artworks are as follows: Sol Lewitt, *Wall Drawing #337: Two part drawing. The wall is divided vertically into two parts. Each part is divided horizontally and vertically into four equal parts. 1st part: Lines in four directions, one direction in each quarter. 2nd part: Lines in four directions, superimposed progressively* and *Wall Drawing #338: Two part drawing. The wall is divided vertically into two parts. Each part is divided horizontally and vertically into four equal parts. 1st part: Lines in four directions, one direction in each quarter. 2nd part: Lines in four directions, superimposed progressively.* (1971), Coloured Pencil, Dimensions Variable. John Kaldor Family Collection at the Art Gallery of New South Wales.

[11]   Art Gallery New South Wales, "Sol Lewitt," http://www.artgallery.nsw.gov.au/ work/351.2011/ (accessed May 19, 2012)

[12]   Representation of Richard Prince's *Untitled (hippie drawing)* (2000-2005) was fabricated in China at fifty percent scale of the original in mixed media on paper and later framed for presentation. The Art Gallery of New South Wales website does not provide a narrative description about the artwork or artist. Details of the original artwork are as follows: Richard Prince, *Untitled (hippie drawing)* (2000-2005), Ink and Synthetic Polymer Paint on Paper, 101.3 x 76.2cm sheet; 132.3 x 107.0 x 4.5 cm frame. John Kaldor Family Collection at the Art Gallery of New South Wales.

Endnotes:
Alive and Well: The Role of the Author / Mary Coyne

ⁱ Keith Aoki, "(Intellectual) Property and Sovereignty: Notes toward a Cultural Geography of Authorship," *Stanford Law Review* 48 (1996): 1293-1355.

ⁱⁱ Walter Benjamin, "The Author as Producer (1934)", reprinted in *Art in Theory 1900-2000: An Anthology of Changing Ideas*, ed. Charles Harrison and Paul Wood (Oxford, UK: Blackwell, 1992), 483-489.

ⁱⁱⁱ Roland Barthes, "The Death of the Author," *In Image, Music, Text* by Roland Barthes, trans. S. Heath (London: Fontana, 1977), 142-148.

^{iv} Barthes, 145. Barthes' linguistically based ideas regarding the dependent nature of signs originated with the late nineteenth century French poet, Stéphane Mallarmé, whose work was closely studied by Jaqcues Derrida. Derrida's *Speech and Phenomena* (1967) and *Of Grammatology* (1967) further unfixed the sign, and questioned the work's and the author's presence.

^v Foucault "What is an Author." In *The Foucault Reader*, ed. Paul Rabinow (New York: Pantheon Books, 1984), 105.

^{vi} Benjamin, in describing the current condition of the Soviet Press indicates an undeniable reality of the twenty-first century. "The reader is indeed always ready to become a writer, that is to say, someone who describes or even who prescribes. As an expert—even if not a professional, but only a job occupant—he gains entrance to authorship." Benjamin, 483-489.

^{vii} Antonio Calcagno, "Foucault and Derrida: the Question of Empowering the Disempowering the Author," *Humanities Studies* 32 (2009), 33-51.

^{viii} Foucault, 118.

^{ix} George Segal's anonymous plaster of Paris statures abet tragically employ aspects of daily urban life, leaving the viewers feel as un-individual as the subject of their gaze.

^x Isabelle Graw, *High Price* (Berlin: Sternberg Press, 2010).

^{xi} Foucault identifies the origin of the role of the modern author as originating in eighteenth century Europe when a focus on the factual data within texts and the intent to prosecute those whose ideas were identified as potentially harmful prioritized attaching an individual to the text (108). Heightened international security post 9/11, and the recent persecution of artists like Ai Wei Wei should bring new focus to this aspect of authorship that makes authors victims as opposed to wielders of control.

[xii] Chad Bray and Jennifer Maloney, "Fake Pollock Alledged," *The Wall Street Journal*, December 3, 2011, under "NY Crime," http://online.wsj.com/article/SB1 0001424052970204826704577074840561587760.html (accessed May 26, 2012).

[xiii] The practice of connoisseurship, reaching its high in the mid-nineteenth century consisted of closely observing the formal qualities of the work of art, the style in which it was completed and researching its known provenance in order to establish a validation of authenticity. The approval of a connoisseur became progressively more important as forged copies of ancient and Renaissance sculpture began flooding western Europe at this time.

Since 1983 the J. Paul Getty Museum in Los Angeles has been undecided about the authenticity of a supposed sixth-century B.C. *korus*. The piece remains of display despite the uncertainty of its provenance, indicating that for the Getty, the piece's form as an example of large scale Classical figurative sculpture remains intact. Michael Kimmelman, "Absolutely Real? Absolutely Fake?," *The New York Times*, August 4, 1991.

Endnotes:
In the Eye of the Beholder: Artistic Value and Censorship | Andrea Bronte

[1]   This essay has been excerpted from a previous unpublished essay dated 2011.

[2]   Thomas Hoving, "Chapter 31: The Getty Wars," Artnet.com, http://www.artnet.com/magazineus/features/hoving/artful-tom-chapter-thirty-one6-12-09.asp (accessed November 15, 2011).

[3]   Marion True, "A kouros at the Getty Museum," *The Burlington Magazine*, January 1987, 6.

[4]   The J. Paul Getty Museum, "Statue of a Kouros," The J. Paul Getty Museum, http://www.getty.edu/art/gettyguide/artObjectDetails?artobj=12908 (accessed November 1, 1011).

[5]   Ibid.

[6]   Hoving, "Chapter 31: The Getty Wars."

[7]   Steven C. Dubin, "Incivilities in Civil(-ized) Places: 'Culture Wars,' in Comparative Perspective," in *A Companion to Museum Studies*, ed. Sharon Macdonald (Massachusetts: Blackwell Publishing, 2006), 479.

[8]   Teri Horton, Tod M. Volpe and Ben Heller. *Who the #$&%% Is Jackson Pollock?*, DVD. Directed by Harry Moses. (New York, NY: Picturehouse, 2006).

[9]   Cindy Hill, "The Legal Perspective: A Response to Teri Horton's Comment Regarding Authentication." The Fine Art Registry, http://www.fineartregistry.com/articles/hill_cindy/legal_perspective_12-28-2006.php1 (accessed November 15 2011).

[10]   Joseph Leo Koerner and Lisbet Rausing, "Value," in *Critical Terms for Art History*, eds. Robert S. Nelson and Richard Shiff (Chicago: The University of Chicago Press, 2003), 419.

[11]   Ibid., 421.

[12]   Randy Kennedy, "Could Be a Pollock; Must Be a Yarn." *The New York Times*. November 15, 2011.

[13]   Horton, *Who the #$&%% Is Jackson Pollock?*

[14]   Thomas Hoving, "The Fate of The $5 Pollock." Artnet.com, http://www.artnet.com/magazineus/features/hoving/hoving11-6-08.asp (accessed November 15, 2011).

[15]   Donald Preziosi, "Art History and Museology: Rendering the Visible Legible," in *A Companion to Museum Studies*, ed. Sharon Macdonald (Massachusetts: Blackwell Publishing, 2006), 52,53.

[16] Fraser, "It's Art When I Say It's Art, or...." in *Museum Highlights: The Writings of Andrea Fraser*, ed. Alexander Alberro (Massachusetts: The MIT Press, 2005), 39.

[17] Horton, *Who the #$&% Is Jackson Pollock?*

[18] *60 Minutes*, "A Thrift-Shop Jackson Pollock Masterpiece?" February 11, 2009, http://www.cbsnews.com/stories/2007/05/03/60minutes/main2758110.shtml?tag=currentVideoInfo;videoMetaInfo (accessed November 15, 2011).

[19] Horton, *Who the #$&% Is Jackson Pollock?*

[20] Ibid.

[21] Fraser, "It's Art When I Say It's Art, or...," 43.

[22] Amelia Jones, "Every Man Knows Where and How Beauty Gives Him Pleasure," in *The Art of Art History: A Critical Anthology*, ed. Donald Preziosi (New York: Oxford University Press, 2009), 375.

[23] Brian O'Doherty, *Inside the White Cube: The Ideology of the Gallery Space.* (California: UC Press, 1999).

[24] Tony Bennett, "The Birth of the Museum." *The Birth of the Museum: history, theory, politics.* (New York: Routledge, 2005), 95.

[25] Fraser, "It's Art When I Say It's Art, Or....," 41.

[26] Emory Elliott, "Introduction: Cultural Diversity and the Problem of Aesthetics," in *Aesthetics in a Multicultural Age*, eds. Emory Elliott, Louis Freitas Caton, H. Jeffrey Rhyne (New York: Oxford University Press, 2002), 9.

[27] Amelia Jones, "Every Man Knows Where and How Beauty Gives Him Pleasure," 376.

Abstract painting (812) by Gerhard Richter 1994, 2012
Oil on canvas (stretched)
121.92 x 96.52 cm

Frise by Daniel Buren 1979, 2012
Oil on canvas (stretched)
5.08 x 12.7 cm

Painting (1) by Michael Landy 2007, 2012
Oil on canvas (stretched)
83.82 x 116.84 cm

New York triptych by Francis Alÿs 1995-1996, 2012
Oil on canvas (stretched)
6.98 x 8.89 cm
45.72 x 58.42 cm
30.38 x 38.1 cm

siebterjulizweitausendundnull by Ugo Rondinone 2000 and Stephan Hawking and the illusion of size by Dale Frank 2001, 2012
Oil on canvas (rolled)
121.92 x 7.62 cm

Untitled (Audio Tour) from The Unauthorised Collection of John Kaldor, 2012
Digital recording
Dimensions variable
Voice: Tonya Dantuma

Untitled (Catalog) from The Unauthorised Collection of John Kaldor, 2012
Mixed media
Dimensions variable
Writing: Andrea Bronte, Mary Coyne, Joseph G. Cruz

Untitled (Interview) from The Unauthorised Collection of John Kaldor, 2012
Digital Video
3:12 minutes (continuous)
Videography: Aaron Giesel
Acting: Scott Rodgers

Untitled (Notes) from The Unauthorised Collection of John Kaldor, 2012
Mixed media on paper
Dimensions variable

Untitled by Frank Stella 1965, 2012
Oil on canvas (stretched)
82.8 x 162.56 cm

Untitled (hippie drawing) by Richard Prince 2000-2005, 2012
Mixed media on paper (framed)
50.8 x 38.1 cm.

Wall drawing #337: two part wall drawing. The wall is divided vertically into two parts. Each part is divided horizontally and vertically into four equal parts. 1st part: lines in four directions, one direction in each quarter. 2nd part: lines in four directions, superimposed progressively and Wall drawing #338: two part wall drawing. The wall is divided vertically into two parts. Each part is divided horizontally and vertically into four equal parts. 1st part: lines in four directions, one direction in each quarter. 2nd part: lines in four directions, superimposed progressively by Sol Lewitt 1971, 2012
Oil on canvas (stretched)
20.32 x 30.48 cm

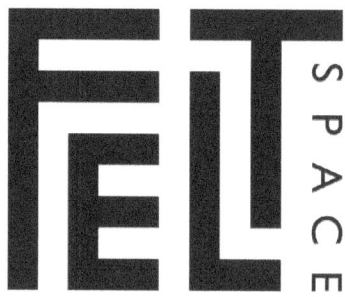

.

www.ingramcontent.com/pod-product-compliance
Lightning Source LLC
Chambersburg PA
CBHW021932170526
45157CB00005B/2290